Jefferson County
R.J. Bailar Public Library

DEC 0 5 2019

375 South Water Street
Monticello, FL 32344
(850) 342-0205

SPOTLIGHT ON THE AMERICAN INDIANS OF CALIFORNIA

THE MONO

GABRIEL MERRICK

NEW YORK

Published in 2018 by The Rosen Publishing Group, Inc.
29 East 21st Street, New York, NY 10010

Copyright © 2018 by The Rosen Publishing Group, Inc.

All rights reserved. No part of this book may be reproduced in any form without permission in writing from the publisher, except by a reviewer.

Editor: Theresa Morlock
Book Design: Michael Flynn
Interior Layout: Reann Nye

Photo Credits: Cover, pp. 9, 13, 23 Courtesy of the Library of Congress; p. 5 Radoslaw Lecyk/Shutterstock.com; p. 6 Galyna Andrushko/Shutterstock.com; p. 7 Tom Grundy/Shutterstock.com; p. 10 Gabriele Maltinti/Shutterstock.com; p. 11 Zack Frank/Shutterstock.com; p. 15 ZUMA Press, Inc./Alamy Stock Photo; p. 17 Barnes Ian/Shutterstock.com; p. 18 trekandshoot/Shutterstock.com; p. 19 www.sandatlas.org/Shutterstock.com; p. 21 https://commons.wikimedia.org/wiki/File:Photograph_with_text_of_acorn_cache_of_the_Mono_Indians,_California._This_is_from_a_survey_report_of_Fresno_and..._-_NARA_-_296296.jpg; pp. 24–25 Fototeca Storica Nazionale./Hulton Archive/Getty Images; p. 27 Underwood Archives/Archie Photos/Getty Images; p. 29 https://commons.wikimedia.org/wiki/File:Photograph_with_text_of_a_Mono_couple_living_near_Northfork,_California._This_is_from_a_survey_report_of_Fresno_and..._-_NARA_-_296289.jpg.

Library of Congress Cataloging-in-Publication Data

Names: Merrick, Gabriel, author.
Title: The Mono / Gabriel Merrick.
Description: New York : PowerKids Press, [2018] | Series: Spotlight on the American Indians of California | Includes index.
Identifiers: LCCN 2017021324| ISBN 9781538324813 (pbk. book) | ISBN 9781538324820 (6 pack) | ISBN 9781538324783 (library bound book)
Subjects: LCSH: Mono Indians--Juvenile literature.
Classification: LCC E99.M86 M47 2018 | DDC 305.897/457--dc23
LC record available at https://lccn.loc.gov/2017021324

Manufactured in China

CPSIA Compliance Information: Batch #BW18PK For further information contact Rosen Publishing, New York, New York at 1-800-237-9932.

CONTENTS

WHO ARE THE MONO?. 4
LIVING OFF THE LAND 6
WHAT THEY ATE. 8
WHERE THEY LIVED 10
SOCIAL STRUCTURE. 14
LEADERSHIP 16
WARFARE. 18
RELIGION 20
ARTS AND CRAFTS. 22
SPANISH ARRIVAL 24
A CHANGING WORLD. 26
THE MONO AND THE UNITED STATES. . . .28
THE MONO TODAY. 30
GLOSSARY 31
INDEX 32
PRIMARY SOURCE LIST. 32
WEBSITES. 32

CHAPTER ONE

WHO ARE THE MONO?

The Mono are a prominent California people. There are two main divisions of the Mono—the eastern and the western groups. The easterners include the Owens Valley Paiute-Shoshone and the Mono Lake Northern Paiute. The Western Mono are also called the Monache.

No one is certain how many Mono people were living in California when the first European explorers arrived in North America around 1492. Experts have suggested that there may have been between 3,000 and 5,000 Mono in the region.

The Mono nation has always worked hard to survive in the face of natural and man-made challenges. This has been especially true since the arrival of large numbers of outsiders, which began around 1850. Despite the demands placed on them by many generations of invaders, these proud people have continued their fight for justice and the survival of their beliefs and **customs**.

Mono Lake is a beautiful and important part of the region that once belonged to the Mono people. In the center of the lake is an ancient volcanic cone, crusted with curious salt formations.

CHAPTER TWO

LIVING OFF THE LAND

The Mono people have lived in California for thousands of years. The Mono's mountainous homeland in eastern California and western Nevada is made up of several geographic regions. The western border of the territory is the Sierra Nevada. This mountain chain includes the tallest place in the Mono's territory, Mount Whitney, which towers 14,494 feet (4,418 m) above sea level.

Mount Whitney is one of the highest peaks in the United States. The mountain wildlife provided the Mono with many important resources.

    Because their lands cover a huge geographic range, the Mono experienced very different types of weather, from very hot summers to very cold winters. Wherever they lived, the Mono depended on gathering wild plants, hunting, and fishing for everything they ate. Beyond this, the patterns of their way of life varied according to where they lived. The groups that made their homes on the western slopes of the Sierra Nevada had more water, plants, and animals than their eastern neighbors.

CHAPTER THREE
WHAT THEY ATE

The Mono's **environment** was filled with things they could eat. Throughout the region there were bighorn sheep, deer, bears, antelope, and other creatures. The Mono also ate smaller creatures, including rabbits, snakes, and birds. The streams and lakes were home to many kinds of fish. The Mono's territory could provide hundreds of appetizing plant-based foods, including nuts, seeds, and edible roots such as wild onions.

Mono women were responsible for preparing food. They used several different **techniques** and tools to do so. They often ground plants, roots, and nuts into flour or powder using stone tools. Baskets and **ceramic** bowls were used to cook soups and stews. Some Mono cooks used earth ovens to roast food. The Mono also preserved meat and fish by smoking them. Mono cooks used every part of the plant or animal they prepared. Nothing was wasted.

This photo, taken in 1924, shows a cooking area in a Mono village.

CHAPTER FOUR

WHERE THEY LIVED

The Mono shifted their settlements seasonally to take advantage of the wild foods available during different months. The people who lived in the drier eastern highlands had to move the most. During the summers, many groups moved to cooler higher regions. During the winters, these communities found shelter in the warmer valleys.

California's landscape varies greatly in terms of elevation, climate, and resources.

Mono villages were located at elevations of 500 to 10,000 feet (152 to 3,048 m). Some Mono groups discovered that the land halfway between the peaks and lower valleys had the most food resources. These types of areas are known as **transitional** life zones. In these places, the climate has less dramatic seasonal swings.

Since the Mono moved so often, they didn't collect much property. Everything had to be carried on their backs to the next village site. The average Mono community moved to sites along a trail about 40 miles (64 km) long.

The fact that natural resources were spread out over a large area limited the size of Mono villages. A community that lived in a place with abundant food rarely had more than 50 people. Some settlements only had one family.

When food was abundant, communities of all sizes would temporarily come together. These were happy times when feasts, special ceremonies, and games occurred. These periods also allowed the Mono to meet with their relatives and friends. After the hunts and harvests, the larger group would divide into smaller communities, which would head out separately.

The Mono built houses with round floor plans. The upper part of the house often looked like a dome. Some houses were cone shaped and some were built inside shallow pits. These structures were 6 to 20 feet (1.8 to 6.1 m) across. Walls were made of rocks, bark, reeds, and grass.

This photograph of a traditional Mono home was taken in 1924.

CHAPTER FIVE

SOCIAL STRUCTURE

The family was the smallest group in Mono society. In most families, the oldest man had the final word on decisions and work assignments. Some men, including village leaders, married several women. Marriages were often arranged by parents. Most villagers married members of other Mono settlements, but the Western Mono often married their Yokut or Miwok neighbors.

Most Mono belonged to a particular clan. These people believed that their families shared a single animal ancestor, such as an eagle, mountain lion, or coyote. When a person was born, they joined their father's clan. In some Mono communities, several clans living together in one village were divided into two parts. These social divisions helped the Mono keep track of who did what work.

The village was the largest social unit. Every Mono village had its own political leader or chief.

This woman is weaving a basket. Her craft will be used for a display in the Mono exhibit at the Yosemite Museum in Yosemite, California.

CHAPTER SIX

LEADERSHIP

Mono chiefs were usually members of the eagle clan. Some were chosen to lead because of their abilities, and others were chosen because their fathers had been leaders. Some chiefs had helpers who served as messengers and advisers. Chiefs received special gifts from their followers. However, they gave these objects back to the community during times of trouble or religious celebrations. Although chiefs provided leadership, the Mono basically thought of everyone in their society as equals.

Most Mono settlements also had people who worked as part-time religious leaders and doctors. These people kept objects and performed **rituals** thought to have special powers. These holy men had special dreams in which they were given **supernatural** powers by spirits or ancestors. Doctors were respected by all the members of their societies. Many common people feared them because they believed the doctors could use their powers to hurt their enemies.

The Mono didn't have a structured government system. In most of the Mono territory, each village claimed the areas where its people hunted, fished, and gathered.

CHAPTER SEVEN

WARFARE

Wars sometimes broke out when one community accused another of having religious leaders who had used supernatural forces to hurt them. However, the Mono people rarely turned to warfare as a way of solving their problems. Of all the people who lived close to the Mono, only the Washoe were thought of as dangerous. When Mono warriors went out to battle, the village chief usually led the men. The fighters relied on spears and bows and arrows as weapons. The lack of armor, shields, and other protective equipment reflected the Mono's limited interest in warfare.

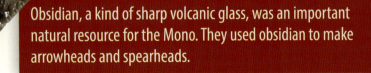

Obsidian, a kind of sharp volcanic glass, was an important natural resource for the Mono. They used obsidian to make arrowheads and spearheads.

NATURAL OBSIDIAN

    Within Mono villages, family conflicts sometimes ended in violence. These struggles were usually short, and few people were hurt or killed. It was very unusual for an entire community or settlement to be destroyed. The village chiefs worked hard to keep this kind of violence from getting out of hand.

CHAPTER EIGHT

RELIGION

The Mono's religious beliefs helped them make sense of the world around them. These beliefs also provided them with important values they could follow to live as good people. Most of the Mono's religious ceremonies were held to keep the people's lives and the world in balance.

Three of the most important Mono ceremonies were the bear dance, the rattlesnake dance, and the annual mourning ceremony. Many religious holidays were tied to the annual cycle of food harvests. During these events, the Mono offered thanks for the community's survival.

When the Mono celebrated, they made music and danced. Their instruments included rattles, whistles, and flutes. They also made art. The Mono sometimes scratched designs onto large stones. These images are called petroglyphs. Some experts believe that these symbols were created during religious ceremonies. Many places with rock art are sacred to American Indian people.

This picture taken around 1920 shows a Mono couple beside a large basket of acorns after the harvest.

CHAPTER NINE

ARTS AND CRAFTS

The Mono used natural resources to create crafts with beautiful designs. Mono women made baskets in many different shapes. Some were used as jars, fans, dishes, cradles, or boxes. To make different patterns, the women wove certain kinds of grasses and tree shoots together into a single basket. By changing the materials, they created hundreds of different designs. Cooking baskets were woven so tightly they could hold liquids.

Most Mono groups also made pottery. They dug clay out of streambeds and hillsides and combined it with sand and water. The wet mixture was formed into long, snakelike pieces. These pieces were slowly coiled together to form pots and jars. The pots were dried in the sun and then stacked in a pit to be heated in a fire. After they cooled, they were ready to use. The Mono traded their creations with their western neighbors.

This Lake Mono woman, photographed in 1924, is holding a basket she made.

CHAPTER TEN

SPANISH ARRIVAL

In 1540, the first Europeans reached Southern California. More than 200 years would pass before the first Spanish colony was created at San Diego. During this period, the European explorers never reached the lands of the Mono, who were hidden by the immense geographic **barriers** of the Sierra Nevada and the Mojave Desert.

Although the explorers didn't come into direct contact with the Mono, they introduced a variety of diseases to the Americas. These illnesses spread inland as people interacted through trade and animals and insects traveled with the seasons. The diseases killed many American Indian people and most likely affected the Mono. During this time, the populations of some American Indian nations dropped by as much as 90 percent. That means that nine out of every ten Mono may have died of European diseases between 1520 and 1769.

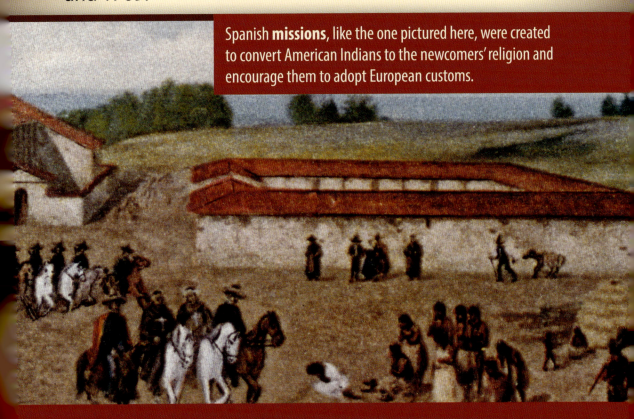

Spanish **missions**, like the one pictured here, were created to convert American Indians to the newcomers' religion and encourage them to adopt European customs.

CHAPTER ELEVEN

A CHANGING WORLD

The Spanish established 21 missions and 4 military bases on the coast of California between 1769 and 1821. Although the Mono didn't have direct contact with them, the Spanish presence in California brought about major changes that affected the Mono's way of life. Old trading relationships between American Indian nations were replaced by a new European trade system. European plants and animals spread inland, often damaging the environment.

Although the invaders introduced many horrors, their arrival also brought opportunities. American Indians who didn't want to join the missions escaped into Mono territories. They brought new ideas that the Mono used to improve their hunting and gathering. Some groups experimented with growing crops and hunting livestock such as sheep and cattle. American Indians began to use horses and some Spanish tools and weapons. During the early 1820s, some explorers began to make contact with the Mono.

After 1835, trade involving European goods increased greatly. Steel knives, wool blankets, guns, and horses were more readily available, even for remote people like the Mono.

CHAPTER TWELVE

THE MONO AND THE UNITED STATES

Between 1846 and 1848, Mexico and the United States fought a war over territory in the western part of North America. When the war ended, the territory of California was granted to the United States. In 1848, the discovery of gold in the Sierra Nevada brought a huge number of newcomers to the region. Within a few years, the miners began to move south and east in search of more gold.

In 1852, gold was discovered in Mono lands. The Mono's territory was soon filled with invaders who thought that American Indians should be killed or forced to move away. The invaders often murdered entire American Indian communities. Some Mono were forced to live as beggars or work as slaves. The mining towns polluted the land and water. Many Mono people resisted the invaders, but for the most part their efforts were unsuccessful.

Many Mono people were forced to change their lifestyle in order to survive. This Mono couple was photographed in Norfolk, California, in 1920.

CHAPTER THIRTEEN

THE MONO TODAY

Few people experienced more changes to their homeland than the Mono. For many years, the United States government created policies and programs designed to eliminate American Indians as a community. As a result of these policies, the Mono suffered huge losses. Still, their will to survive as a people has never ended.

During the early 1900s, some **reservations** were created for the Mono people. Unfortunately, the Mono have struggled to maintain control of these reservations, some of which have been eliminated by the U.S. government.

The people of the Mono nation are working hard to create jobs and reclaim their **heritage**. The Mono continue to struggle to save their traditional sacred places, such as Coso Hot Springs. By continuing their ancient customs and making their own **unique** contributions to the modern world, the Mono's existence will benefit all the people of the United States.

GLOSSARY

barrier (BAA-ree-uhr) Something that blocks something from passing.

ceramic (suh-RAH-mik) Made of clay that is then heated to a very high temperature so that it hardens.

custom (KUS-tum) An action or way of behaving that is traditional among the people in a certain group or place.

environment (en-VY-run-ment) The natural world around us.

heritage (HEHR-uh-tijh) The traditions and beliefs that are part of the history of a group or nation.

mission (MIH-shun) A community established by a church for the purpose of spreading its faith.

reservation (reh-zuhr-VAY-shun) Land set aside by the government for specific American Indian nations to live on.

ritual (RIH-choo-uhl) A religious ceremony, especially one consisting of a series of actions performed in a certain order.

supernatural (soo-pur-NAH-chur-uhl) Unable to be explained by science or the laws of nature.

technique (tek-NEEK) A particular skill or ability that someone uses to perform a job.

transitional (tran-ZIH-shuh-nuhl) Having to do with passage from one state, stage, or place to another.

unique (yoo-NEEK) Special or different from anything else.

INDEX

B
baskets, 8, 20, 22

C
chief, 14, 16, 18, 19
clan, 14, 16
Coso Hot Springs, 30

E
European, 4, 24, 25, 26

G
gold, 28

M
Mexico, 28
missions, 25, 26
Miwok, 14
Mojave Desert, 24
Monache, 4
Mono Lake, 4
Mono Lake Northern Paiute, 4

N
Nevada, 6
Norfolk, 28

O
obsidian, 18, 19
Owens Valley Paiute-Shoshone, 4

P
petroglyph, 20
pottery, 22

R
reservations, 30
ritual, 16

S
San Diego, 24
Sierra Nevada, 6, 7, 24, 28
Spanish, 24, 25, 26

V
villages, 8, 11, 12, 14, 16, 19

W
Washoe, 18
Western Mono, 4, 14
Whitney, Mount, 6, 7

Y
Yokut, 14
Yosemite, 14

PRIMARY SOURCE LIST

Page 9
Mono summer kitchen. Photograph. Taken by Edward S. Curtis. August 5, 1924. Now kept at the Library of Congress, Prints and Photographs Division, Washington, D.C.

Page 13
A Mono home. Photograph. Taken by Edward S. Curtis. August 5, 1924. Now kept at the Library of Congress, Prints and Photographs Division, Washington, D.C.

Page 23
A Lake Mono basket-maker. Photograph. Taken by Edward S. Curtis. ca. 1924. Now kept at the Library of Congress, Prints and Photographs Division, Washington, D.C.

WEBSITES

Due to the changing nature of Internet links, PowerKids Press has developed an online list of websites related to the subject of this book. This site is updated regularly. Please use this link to access the list: www.powerkidslinks.com/saic/mono